MANAGING FINANCES DURING A CRISIS

Planning and Managing Your BUSINESS And PERSONAL Finances During DIFFICULT and GOOD Times

By

Saurabh Maheshwari

This book is dedicated to:

My Parents and My wife who have been my pillar of strengths through-out my life. They have given me the freedom to take my decisions, make my mistakes and yet have remained the rocks on whose foundations I have built my life.

Thank You Papa.

Thank You Mummy

Thank you Megha.

Our other Books

NO-NONSENSE BUSINESS TURNAROUNDS
By – Saurabh Maheshwari and Ram Parthasarathy

More often than not, we see our businesses facing challenges - financial and economic - and struggling for survival. More often than not, we are looking for help but are unsure where to go or whom to ask. If You and your business are struggling to survive and every single month is a struggle to survive, then this book is for you.

Available at:
https://www.amazon.in/dp/B087D587XT (India)
https://www.amazon.com/dp/B087D587XT (USA)

Also Available as an ebook across all Geographies where Kindle is available.

Table of Contents

Introduction

Thank you for picking up this book.

I am writing this book at the time when there is lockdown across the world over Corona Virus (COVID-19) and the world economy is in a state of shock. The news flows across financial channels have the following theme –

- *Stock markets across the world are down 20%-50% from peaks,*
- *The trade has come to a standstill,*
- *Governments across the world have launched trillion-dollar rescue packages.*
- *Businessmen are wondering when will the businesses and cash flows start again,*
- *Informal sector / contract workers / Daily wage earners / taxi drivers are losing their jobs and incomes,*
- *People still with jobs are fearing that a huge round of job cuts are coming.*
- *30% to 50% of all Small Businesses are expected to shut down.*

The world has changed indeed.

Wouldn't it be nice to have a financial fortress which can withstand all that life can throw at you – financial and economic shocks, sudden loss of income, sudden large medical expense, or anything else which may come your way? Wouldn't it be nice to be prepared for the storms and not worry about them when they come? Wouldn't it be nice to not worry about your finance all the time? Wouldn't it be nice to know what your future financial situation will look like? Wouldn't you want to assess and understand if you are going in the right direction?

Whether you are the owner of a large business responsible for the 200 staff that you have or just a salaried person taking care of the finances of your family, it is times of crisis and difficulties that really test the robustness and strength of your financial fortress.

It is during these times, that you really need to ensure that the storms do not blow away your house along with it. Yes, there will be clear skies very soon, but your business and your personal finances need to get through these difficult times first.

You may think that I have so and so amount saved up. Hence, I know my financial position. My only submission here is that you know your financial holdings, but are you also aware of how it changes on a daily / weekly / monthly basis? Everything you do – eating out, saving, earning, spending affects this financial position. Every amount you earn (whether as salary or as fees or profits) affects your financial position.

What you own, the Debts you have, your income, your expenses, your investments, and a million little items – All impact your financial position.

Whew, that's a lot of moving parts and a lot of information. But information becomes actionable data when it is arranged in a logical manner and is updated frequently. And actionable data is useful only when you take some action basis the data, when you do something with it.

This book will do exactly that. Through this book, I will give you practical pointers to the steps you need to take to ensure that your finances survive this hurricane. I will also give you simple and effective way to assess your financial health. Also, this book will give you action steps to further strengthen your financial fortress so that you are better prepared for the storms that will surely come in the future. This book will give you a system to put all the information on one side and get actionable data on the other side. We do this by in 3 steps / parts –

Part I – Assessment - This will give you the framework to assess your present financial situation – applicable for both Business Owners assessing their business and for individuals assessing their personal finances. Once we know where we are, then we can decide on what to do to improve it.

Part II – Action Points - Depending on the assessment done in part I, this section will give business owners steps and measures to take to strengthen their business finances. This will give you broad action steps, which you, as a business owner can take and customize it as per its own need. It will also give individuals the tools to improve their financial well-being. Since, generally, the income of individuals is fairly inelastic grows only linearly, the pointers here will differ greatly from what a business owner can do.

We would suggest that you go through the assessment part thoroughly and identify the present situation of your finances (whether personal or Business). Once you identify the particular situation, you have the choice to go straight to that part in the book for very concise tips and solutions. However, we strongly suggest that you go through the rest of the book too for other ideas and thoughts which will surely ignite the way you think about your personal finances.

Who am I?

I have been a banker for the initial 11 years of my career (doing retail and corporate loans) assessing the creditworthiness of borrowers, handling large teams and geographies. For the last 7 years, I am an entrepreneur employing 8 people, advising companies on their Balance Sheets, Finances and helping them raise institutional money. In these 18 years, I have closely seen companies and individuals grow from nothing to great businesses and wealth and also the reverse – Large businesses and wealthy individuals losing it all. I have also closely seen companies and individuals in financial doldrums achieve spectacular turnarounds. This book is a distillation of all my work experience, mixed with my own personal experiences and learnings.

What this book is not about

This book is not about suggesting avenues and instruments to save and invest. This book will also not tell you how to magically pay off your debt. This book is not about retirement planning. We may touch upon a few terms and financials instruments throughout the book, but this book will not give you strategies or guidance to invest in stock markets, real estate, bonds, etc. This book is also certainly not a magic pill which will solve all your financial issues. But this book will certainly tell you about what ails your financial situation and what can be the possible avenues to take to solve the issues. This book will become the foundation of your financial planning and using the concepts given here you can prepare a plan to put your house in order.

However, before taking any action basis the content of this book, we would advise you to consult with you Accountant and Financial Advisors and also run it through your family members and people you trust.

Let's start.

Saurabh Maheshwari

April 2020

PART I: Assessing Your Financial Situation

The first thing to start any journey is know where you are. The same is also true for your financial life also. Whether you are a large or a small business or you are a salaried person, you absolutely NEED to know where you stand financially.

There are a multitude of assessment tools available in the industry for measuring your savings rate, your net worth, the value of your portfolio, the real estate in your books, your debts, etc. There are retirement calculators, investment calculators, debt repayment calculators, and a plethora of tools available – Just do a quick google search. There are programs on early elimination of debt and being debt free (Even if it means selling everything you have) and then there are programs on the Power of Leverage and using Other People's Money. There are programs on building wealth through the equity markets and there are those on real estate. The list is endless and the information is so much that if we start going through it all, we will not be able to consume it all in our present lifetime.

Are the tools above useful – Yes, all of these tools are useful in their own way, but they do not give you the complete and holistic picture of your business or personal finances in an easy to understand and practical way. They do not tell the ailment or they do not tell you about the key area which you have to tackle first.

Through this chapter, we will give you tools to organize your information in a logical and sequential manner so that with once glance at the final output, you will know exactly where you are and what is the biggest problem you need to face first, which is that key thing which you need to focus on first.

So, without further delay, whether you are a small or large business, or you are in individual, let's get organizing your financial information.

All of your financial information can be divided into the following 2 categories -

1. Cash Flows
2. Assets and Liabilities

Let's take them one at a time. Let's dive right in.

Chapter One: Cash Flows

Cash flows – That's the holy grail. The starting Point. Cash flows are a product of 2 things – Inflows and Outflows. There is no further complication. It does not need any explanation and if you have done primary grade Math (which I am sure you have), you will complete this part with ease.

Your Inflows

Cash Inflows as the term says is simply the money you receive regularly every month. You may ask, is it really that simple. The answer is YES, It is really that simple

Key points being **Regular** and **Money received in the Bank**.

Now that we have defined what is the cash inflow, let's get to measuring it. To measure, lets collect all the documents that will tell you what your cash inflow is. The following 2 documents will be needed for you to accurately measure your cash inflows –

1. Bank statements -This will be the absolutely the document which will give you 100% of your inflows. *If it's not coming to the bank, it's not an inflow* – no matter what you think. The only inflow is the money which you get.

2. Refer to Document Number 1.

You do not need your salary slips or any other document to actually measure your cash inflows. Even if you are a businessman, you need just your bank statement to assess what your cash flows are. You do not need a fancy accounting software, you do not need your bills, or any other document to assess your present cash inflows.

Cash inflows is not to be confused with Sales or Monthly Invoices (for business cash flows). The value of invoices you raise has got nothing to do with your cash flows. The only thing that matters and you have to measure is the cash you collect.

But, Saurabh - You may say, I have a small business and I can't collect if I don't invoice. That's True. But look at the situation where you have a substantial amount of bills to collect and no money in bank to fulfill your obligations. You cannot pay your employees their salaries, you cannot pay the debts, you cannot pay the electricity bills. What use will these uncollected invoices be in such a case? So, the most critical thing to measure is the amount you collect every month.

Or, let's look at the case where you get a salary every month. You may say that my salary is much higher than what comes into the bank. The Provident Fund and the Pension Deductions are my own money.

My answer to you will be the same. You have your deductions in terms of Tax, Provident Fund, Pension Deductions etc. before you get a lesser amount deposited to your bank. The Provident Fund Money is your money, but it is not available to use in case of an emergency. You cannot use it to pay for food or to pay your child's school fees or your electricity bills. So, again, the only thing to measure is the money in your bank.

Now that I have convinced you the importance of What you need to do right now is to take a piece of paper and write down all your cash inflows for the last 6 months. There is a format in the pages that follow.

Your inflows may include the following

For A Business owner	For an individual	Applicable for Both
Cash flow from Sales	Net cash from salaries.	Interest on bank balances
	Bonuses	Rental from real estate
		Tax Refunds

		Interest on investments

What not to include in your cash inflows –

1. Income from sale of assets – If you sell your house or that real estate asset, it's going to be a one-time income which you will get only when you are selling that asset. It has not been a part of cash inflow before and will not be a part of inflows later.

2. Any non-regular income – Any inflow which is once in a while is not to be included in the cash flows. Examples include insurance payouts, inheritances, gifts received from relatives, etc.

What we will do immediately now is to take that Bank statement you have downloaded and using the above classifications, write down your personal or business cash flows in the table below.

Once you write down the cash flows, the next thing is to average it all for the last 6 months (just add the six months inflow under that head and divide it by six).

Table 1

Cash Inflows (Last 6 months): -

Cash inflows (Bank Credits only)	Average	Apr	Mar	Feb	Jan	Dec	Nov
Sales							
Salary							
Dividends							

Bonuses							
Bank Interest							
Other Interest							
Other Income							
Total							

Great. Now we have completed the first step of the process and you have a pretty good hang of what your inflows are. For Business Owners, I am sure it has come as a surprise and of course, it may surprise a few individuals too.

Now that we have covered the inflow part, let's go ahead and start working on those outflows too.

Your Outflows

In absolutely simple terms, Outflows are basically everything you have to pay for to keep the home and business running.

If you are an individual, it will include the following: -

- Your household expenses (Money for food, clothing etc.).
- Your loan EMIs – Housing loan, Vehicle loan, etc.
- Recurring expenses like your Broadband or internet bills, Electricity, Society Maintenance, Rent, Maids salaries, fuel, Mobile Phone bills, vehicle repairs, etc.
- Irregular but recurring expenses like travel, holidays, etc.
- Money spent on Gadgets like phones, televisions, gaming consoles, etc.
- Your children's education fees, Bus fees etc.

Some People would want to include savings and Mutual Fund SIPs here too, but I would keep it outside of this list at this point. You should only list your expenses here at this point.

For a Business owner, all the points above apply. After all, he is also running his household and has personal expenses. But in addition, the following expenses also have to be taken care of: -

- Office Rent / Maintenance.
- Staff Salaries and Bonuses.
- Office Expenses like tea, coffee, cleaning, etc.
- Copier Bills.
- Staff Travel Bills.
- Software Expenses.
- Hardware and Equipment Purchases.
- Security Expenses.
- Instalments and Interest payments if there are loans on the business.
- Office Electricity Bills.
- Office internet and telephone Bills.

- Printing and Stationery expenses.
- License fees.
- Marketing and Advertisement Expenses
- Website maintenance and annual hosting fees.
- Email Server fees.
- Cloud Storage and services fees.

The Point to remember here is that only the bank statement may not be enough to capture all these expenses. For this you will have to refer to the following documents in addition to the bank statements –

1. Credit Card statements.
2. Expense Bills and Vouchers.
3. Your account books (provided they are updated)

If You use a software like Tally or QuickBooks, then you can get these reports from the software itself (provided they are set up in details and in the correct manner). But doing this exercise frequently will be of immense help and will give you insights which you may never otherwise have.

Should you include money spent on Equipment's and Assets also in this List?

The simple answer is ABSOLUTELY. Buying a computer also needs money. Buying an asset also needs money.

An Ideal Business will be capable enough to pay for all the assets needed by it out of its cash flows. The only alternative is debt, which is not a bad thing in itself. But, if you should go for it or not, is the subject matter of another book. Let's just say, that for the purposes of this book, we are looking at building your fortress in such a way, that if you so choose, you will be able to pay for all expenses and all your asset purchases from your cash flows.

Use the two tables below as a starting point to list your expenses for the last 6 months. Add item heads if necessary: -

Table 2

Cash Outflows – Personal Expenses (Last 6 months): -

Cash Outflows	*Average*	*Apr*	*Mar*	*Feb*	*Jan*	*Dec*	*Nov*
Basic Household Expenses							
House Rent							
Food							
Grocery							
Eating Out							
Clothing							
Footwear							
Telephone Bills							
Broadband Bills							
Vehicle Repairs							
Fuel							
Society Maintenance							
Cleaning Maid Salary							
Cooking Maid Salary							
Car Cleaner salary							

School and College Fees							
School Bus Charges							
Insurance Premiums							
Other Expenses							
Debt Servicing							
Housing Loan EMI							
Car Loan EMI							
Personal Loan EMI							
Credit Card Interest							
Lifestyle expenses							
Hotels and Holiday expenses							
Air tickets							
Car Hire Expenses							
Train Ticket expenses							
Gifts							
Gadget Purchase - mobile Phone							
Gadget Purchase - Television							
Gadget Purchase – AC							

Gadget Purchase-Gaming Console							
Other Expenses							
Vehicle Purchase/Down-payment							
House Purchase / Down-payment							
Total							

Table 3

Cash Outflows – Business Expenses (Last 6 months): -

Cash Outflows	*Average*	*Apr*	*Mar*	*Feb*	*Jan*	*Dec*	*Nov*
Office Rent							
Staff Salaries and Bonuses.							
Raw Material / Goods Purchased							
Packaging Material purchased							
Transportation charges Paid							
Tea and Coffee Expenses							

Cleaning Expenses							
Copier Bills.							
Staff Travel Bills.							
Software Expenses.							
Equipment Purchases							
Security Expenses.							
Interest on CC/OD							
Installment on Term Loans							
Office Electricity Bills.							
Office internet bills							
Office telephone Bills.							
Printing and Stationery							
License fees.							
Marketing and Advt. Expenses							
Website maintenance & Hosting							
Email Server fees.							
Cloud Storage and services fees.							
Professional Fees – CA							
Professional Fees – lawyer							
Professional Fees – CS							
Taxes and Cess							

Insurance Premiums							
Other expenses							
Other expenses							
Total							

Now that we have the personal and business expenses measured and the average number for last 6 months calculated, you just add them up to get your monthly cash outflow.

Now we are ready for the next step which will complete out assessment of your cash flows – which is calculating your net cash flows.

Net Cash Flows

With inflows and outflows calculated, it's a matter of just filling up the table below: -

Table 4 – Your Net Cash Flows

Net Cash flow	*Average*	*Apr*	*Mar*	*Feb*	*Jan*	*Dec*	*Nov*
Cash Inflows							
Less: Cash outflows *(Personal + Business)*							
Net Cash Flow							

So, what's the final Net Cash Flow number? In a lot of cases it will be negative also.

A positive Cash flow simply indicates that you are able to manage your cash and your inflows are more than your outflows. You are able to meet all your expenses and then have some left over for saving / investing / repaying debts, etc. It's a good place to be in and the larger the number (as a % of total inflows), the better it is.

The negative number here signifies that your expenses are more than your income – which honestly is not sustainable. If it is marginally negative, then you can cut down some expenses to get it into the positive territory. If the number is large, then you will have to do some radical things to change this. And that too urgently.

Spend a few minutes on this and answer the following Questions

- Are you happy with it?
- What were the trends for the last 6 months?
- Will you want to improve it?

- What can you do to improve it? Can you reduce expenses or Increase income?

Now that we have worked out exactly where you are in terms of your cash flows, let's move on to the other part of the puzzle - Your Net Worth.

Chapter Two: Net Worth

According to Investopedia, *"Net worth is the measure of the wealth of an entity, person, or corporation, as well as sectors and countries. Simply, net worth is defined as the difference between assets and liabilities. It is an important metric to gauge a company's health and it provides a snapshot of the firm's current financial position."*

So essentially, we are trying to gauge the current health of your finances.

Also, we per the definition above, there are 2 components of net worth – Assets and Liabilities. Let's get straight into the 2 components.

Assets

An asset is simply anything of value that you own which can be sold for some financial value in the market.

If we look at this there are 3 simple characteristics of the asset-

1. If is something of value.
2. It is something you own.
3. It can be converted to money by selling it.

So, by this definition, the car you own, the house you own, the stocks in your business (which can be sold), the receivables (money to be received from your clients), the television set, etc. are all hard assets. Money in the bank, investment in share markets, fixed deposits, etc. are also examples of assets you own.

Where will you get the details of your assets from?

You normally will get it from the following documents: -

- Bank statements
- Insurance Policy Statements

- Provident Fund passbook
- Pension Statements
- Mutual Fund Statements
- Your share Broking account statement
- Value of real estate can be gauged from the value of similar properties being listed on online property aggregation sites like www.magicbricks.com or www.99acres.com.
- Value of gold and silver can be assessed from the quantity of gold and silver you own and multiplying the same with the value of bullion as on that day. Please ensure that you do not include the making charges of your Jewelry in your calculation. Calculate only the value of gold as per its weight.
- Value of your vehicle can be reasonably estimated from websites like www.cars24.com or www.gaadiwale.com.
- Just look around your home and office and list down all the other assets you own.

Things I would consider assets and a small format for listing your assets is in the table below.

Table 5

Assets

Asset	Present Sale Value (Date: - _____)
Primary Residence	
Primary Office	
Investment Real Estate 1	
Investment Real Estate 2	
Cash Balances	
Bank Balances – Savings account	

Bank Balances – Current Accounts	
Bank Balances – Fixed Deposits	
Stocks / Shares	
Bonds / Company deposits	
Mutual Funds	
Gold / Silver	
Vehicle 1	
Vehicle 2	
Sales Receivables (Uncollected Bills) – suggest a 50% discount.	
Provident Fund Balance (EPF and PPF)	
Pension Scheme Balances	
Present Value of Insurance Policies	
Other Assets 1	
Other Assets 2	
Total Assets	

I personally consider all the other items – Furniture, Computers, Televisions, Clothes, Books, Shoes, Your collection of stamps or currency, Refrigerators, Microwaves, etc. – as zero value. This is because of two primary reasons:

1. You will still need them to function.
2. You will not realize more than 10-15% of the amount you paid for it, essentially nothing too meaningful.

I would strongly urge you also to not consider the same while you calculate your asset values.

There are some items above which you do not have ready access to – like Provident Fund, Pension scheme and Present Value of Insurance Policies. However, you have some restricted access to them as you can withdraw partial amounts with some penalty or borrow against the balances.

I have also included your primary residence and primary office in the list above. Simple reason being you always have the option of selling the same and staying in a rental place for some time. Not a very pleasant option or the recommended option, but an option available nonetheless.

Liabilities

Investopedia definition: *"A liability, in general, is an obligation to, or something that you owe somebody else."*

Merriam Webster defines Liability as *"something for which one is liable".*

So essentially, it's the money you owe to others today. It's the amount which you have to pay for. Nothing More, Nothing Less.

Where will you get the details of your Liabilities from?

You normally will get it from the following documents: -

- Your monthly bills
- Loan statements
- Your email notifications.
- Your account books (if they are maintained properly)
- Your credit card statements

Collect the documents above and fill in the table below.

Table 6 - **Liabilities**

Liability	Current Dues (Date: - _____)
Housing Loan	
Vehicle Loan 1	
Vehicle Loan 2	
Mortgage Loan	
Cash Credit (outstanding amount)	
Credit card outstanding	

Outstanding taxes and govt dues	
Unpaid Bills	
Salaries Payable (outstanding)	
Creditors for Business Purchases (goods and services)	
Unsecured Personal loans	
Unsecured Business Loans	
Advances taken from employers	
Advances from Customers (for businesses)	
Loans from friends and families	
Misc. Loans 1	
Misc. Loans 2	
Total Liabilities	

The total number here will come in as a surprise to most of you. It will certainly be a little or a lot more than what you thought you owed. But liabilities in itself have no meaning until and unless you compare it with assets you own. Having a 50 Lakh loan with 200 lakh in assets is very different from owing 50 Lakh with only 10 Lakh of assets against them.

Let's get quickly to the next step. Putting your assets and liabilities together and finding out your net-worth and relate it to all the other numbers.

Net Worth

Economic Times defines Net Worth as "*Net worth is the difference between the asset and the liability of an individual or a company*".

That's simple!!

You have already worked out your assets and liabilities in pages before this. Use the table below to calculate your Net Worth and we will get down a few small exercises to put the numbers in perspective after that.

Table 7

Net Worth

Net Worth (as on Date_____)	Amount
Assets	
Less: Liabilities	
Net Worth	

Let's just spend some time on this number. I would really want you to internalize this as this number becomes one of the 2 critical numbers that we will keep measuring again and again and again.

What do you see above as your net worth number?

- Is the number positive or negative?
- Is it in line with your expectations?
- Considering the number of years you have been working, Does it really reflect the time you have been working?
- What would you do to improve it? What will be your plan?

Now, we have your cash flow number and your net worth number. These are the only 2 numbers which we should track regularly. The next chapter will tell you how the two connect to each other and it will also give you a few more ratios and numbers which will be of interest to you while working on your finances.

Chapter Three: Your Money Matrix

So, you have been working for the last 20 odd pages, collecting information, giving them a structure, calculating your cash flows and Net Worth. That was a lot of hard work, but it will become the foundation of your financial journey from hereon.

The calculations you have done, the numbers you have got must have been a revelation in themselves. There would have been numbers that would have surprised you, both positively and negatively. In this section I will tell you the following 3 things: -

- The Money Matrix: How are the cash flows and Net Worth Interlinked?
- A few important Liquidity and security numbers which you should know about your finances.
- A bords eye view of your finances.

The Money Matrix

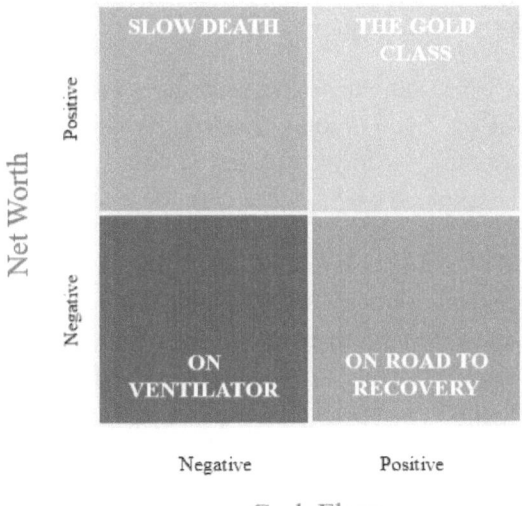

What you need to do now is to place and identify the particular quadrant your finances currently are in. The best way to do it is to take a print out and stick your passport sized photograph in the quadrant where your finances currently are.

I suggest that you spend some time reflecting on your position on the matrix above. Are you happy with it? Would you want to improve it? What will you do immediately? How do you plan to improve things?

I would also strongly suggest that you take a notebook, draw the matrix on it and mark your current financial position in it. Also, below that, write down all your thoughts and emotions at this point of time. Don't edit anything, don't leave anything out, just write it down. The emotions will be very strong and you need to understand that they are just that – emotions, and need an outlet. You will feel much better after getting it out of your system. You have all the power you need to change your circumstances and hence change your emotions.

Taking this journey with your spouse or a close friend or family member will also help – both emotionally and also in terms of keeping you accountable.

Before we get into each quadrant separately and what it means to be in each, I would want you to know (especially if you not in the gold class above and are really worried and scared about your financial future at this point): -

1. **Stay Positive** - Humans have this amazing ability to change around everything. We have heard and possibly also know a few people who have arrived in life Inspite of all the difficulties and all the problems. The list is endless and a quick google search on financial turnaround stories will give you thousands and thousands of examples and all the motivation you need.

2. **Identifying the problem is the first step to solving it** - Now that you know exactly where you are and what is the major issue (negative cash flow or negative net worth can be the only issues), you already know what is to be done to solve this problem.

3. **You do not need to reinvent the wheel** - Remember, all the issues plaguing you have been faced by many other and they have solved it before. Just ask around to see what solutions they had applied. Do a google search, ask your bankers, ask your friends and families for their experiences. You will get a few solutions, take them and adapt them to suit your particular situation. It has been done before.

4. **Don't go through this journey alone** – This will be as much an emotional journey as it will be financial. In this time, having someone in your team, someone who will give you emotional support, someone who can tell you what you are doing wrong and give you an outside perspective can really help. If the person has done it all himself or herself, it will be even better.

So Now you know which quadrant you are in. You also have spent some time thinking about it and have got your thoughts on it written down. Let's refine your thoughts a little more. Let me give you what I believe is the future of a person in each quadrant (Hint: The quadrant's name will tell you this).

Let's get into dissecting the matrix and its components above. Let's start by looking at each axis first.

The Cash Flow Axis

This Photo by Unknown Author is licensed under CC BY-NC-ND

The Best analogy can be that of a leaky bucket. Imagine you are trying to fill a bucket (your bank account) with water (money). There is a tap at the top (your income) which is on. However, the bucket has a few holes and is leaking and the water is flowing out (Expenses). What do you thing will happen here?

If the income is more than expenses, you will be able to fill the bucket and it will remain full. This will happen even when you start with an empty bucket.

However, if the expenses are more than income, then even if you start with a full bucket, it will very soon be empty. That's exactly how positive of negative cash flows impact your personal finances also.

The Net Worth Axis

Net Worth is simply the Net Assets (All your asset less all your liabilities) you have.

And why is Net Worth important? More often than not, it is this judicious mix of assets in your net worth which will help you earn money (like rent, interest and dividends) once your active work life stops.

Also, when situations and things turn bad, Your Net Worth is the cushion that will help you absorb the shocks – financial or otherwise. Take this example when we are in the middle of a global lockdown on account of CORONA virus (it's the year 2020), Most of the income for the world has come to a standstill. If this lockdown continues, then not only will there be mass layoffs, but a lot of businesses will go bankrupt too. In this case, a person or business with assets in his books will be in a better position to tackle these hard times. He can leverage those assets by borrowing against them, he can also sell the asset in case it's a non- core asset and generate liquidity to tide over the problems.

Some of you might say that All assets are not equal. For example, one's real estate investments may not sell at this time. That is whole reason why I believe that your Net Worth should be a judicious mix of assets. Now what should be the proportion of that mix is a topic for another book altogether. Let us just stick to a judicious mix of liquidity along with a healthy investment in long term investments like Real Estate and Businesses.

Hence the simple thought is – The higher the Net Worth, the Better it is for your personal or business finance.

One more thought for you to think on – you should look at the Net Worth as a proportion to your income. If you or your business is are earning 1 Cr per year and have a Net Worth of 1 Cr, then it's really not that great. But if you are earning 10 lacs a year and have a Net Worth of 1 Cr, then you have done a lot of right things.

Let's now get into each quadrant and see what it means. I personally would want to go into the same in the order (my assessment) from the worst quadrant to the best quadrant. Let's get into it straightaway.

Negative Net Worth and Negative Cash Flow

This basically means that as you are bankrupt as your finances stand today.

Picture yourself being in a hole. And now picture the fact that you are still digging every day. What do you think is going to happen? Yes, you will be getting deeper into the hole every single day. You are never come out of this hole if you continue digging. You risk a big chance of this becoming your financial grave.

What being on this quadrant means is that –

1. You do have any assets in your name or you have more liabilities than assets.
2. You are making enough money every month to meet your expenses.

What situations will you face when you are in this.

1. You are deep in debt and it is increasing every single day.
2. Your creditors are hounding you and 90% of the calls you get are collection calls.
3. Every day is a struggle to figure out a way to pay your bills or to push them to the next day.
4. You might be defaulting on your loan installments and interest servicing.
5. If you are a businessman, you do not have enough money to pay the salaries and buy stocks.
6. You are late on your electricity bills.
7. You may or may not have the money to pay for your child's education.
8. You worry about having enough money to get your vehicle repaired.

9. You are looking to borrow more and more money to just tide over present day financial crunch.

These are but a sample of the situations that you will face in this quadrant. There will be variations and more unique situations, but in the end the reason for it will be that you do not enough cash flows to cover your expenses nor are you in a position to sell your assets and get out of the problems (You may not have the assets or they may not be enough to repay the liabilities).

So, Is everything lost? The answer is NO.

Just today I got a whatsapp forward (attributed to Shri Ratan Tata ji, Unconfirmed) stating –

Experts are predicting huge down fall of Economy due to the Corona .

I do not know much about these experts.

But I know for sure that they do not know anything about the value of human motivation and determined efforts.

If experts were to be believed, after the total destruction in 2nd World War Japan had NO future. BUT the same Japan in just 3 decades or so, made US cry at the market place.

If the experts were to be believed, Israel should have been wiped out from the world map by the Arabs, but the fact is different.

As per the rules of Aerodynamics, the Bumble Bee can NOT fly. But it flies, because it does not know the rules of Aerodynamics.

If the experts were to be believed, we should have been nowhere in 83 Cricket World Cup.

If the experts were to be believed Wilma Rudolf, the first American lady to win 4 Olympic Gold in Athletics, should not have been in a position to walk without braces, no question of running.

If the experts were to be believed Arunima Sinha can hardly lead a normal life. But she climbed the Mount Everest.

The corona crisis is no different. I do not have any doubt that, We will defeat the Corona hands down and The Indian Economy will bounce back in a great manner.

The Key message here is obvious – Humans have the capability to turn around the most difficult of things and make spectacular successes out of seemingly unsurmountable difficulties.

I have personally seen spectacular financial turnarounds in my own immediate family and with the clients that I have worked with. In each case, from the depths of financial distress where everyday survival was a challenge, they turned the situation around through sheer hard-work and a little bit of luck.

So, I would request you also to keep the faith. Faith can indeed move mountains and in your case, it will help you reach the pinnacles of financial success.

Positive Net Worth and Negative Cash Flow

I personally call it the slow death quadrant.

Let's take the example of your physical body. You have a small cut through which you are losing a small amount of blood continuously and it is refusing to heal (you have blood pressure and are using medicines which makes it difficult for the wound to heal). You are strong today, but how long do you think you can cope up with it?

How long before the doctor puts you in ICU? Not very long, I can assure you.

Another example of this is the story of the boiling frog - *If you drop a frog in a pot of boiling water, it will of course frantically try to jump out. But if you place it gently in a pot of cold water and turn the heat on low, it will float there merrily. As the water gradually heats up, the frog will not realize that the temperature is rising, and before long, it will boil to death.*

Same is the case with your finances also. You are losing money every month and since you have negative cash flows, you are eroding your Net Worth every single month. Every single day and every single month you are getting weaker and weaker financially. You are borrowing a little more every month to bridge the gap and your credit card outstanding is increasing every month. The debt is increasing at a steady pace This steady erosion in Net worth will put you in financial ICU very-very soon.

The situations which you will typically face if you are in this part of the quadrant will be –

1. Increasing debt levels.
2. Increasing credit card dues.
3. Regular charges for Cheque bounces, late fees and penal interest.
4. Regular stress on cash flows specially during the end of the month.
5. If you are a business, delayed payments of statutory dues and taxes, staff salaries and routine expenses.

6. Increasing payment period to vendors and service providers.

7. Overdrawn or fully drawn working capital limits.

8. Constantly taking on new loans and top up loans against your assets.

People in Businesses in this quadrant normally have a false sense of security enveloping them. They have made these assets, so obviously they have done things right earlier. A lot of them view this as a temporary issue and believe that things will go back to normal on their own. With the next pay raise, the cash flow will be ok. The dropping business sales is due to the economy and will go back to normal soon.

The most important thing to do here is to get out of this false sense of security. You can do this be making your financial numbers (your cash flow sheet and your net worth statement) and look at it very-very closely. This will show you the reality. One more way to do it to speak to your mentor or your family and put these statements in front of them. They will also tell you the issue you are facing.

Having this realization will be the key to you taking necessary steps to take your cash flow from negative to positive territory. This is where you need to be most vigilant and take quick corrective decisions not only to preserve your assets but also to stop and reverse this slow hemorrhage of cash.

Later in the book, we will discuss a few measures you can take to correct this situation.

Negative Net Worth and Positive Cash Flow

This is what I call "Recovering from Cancer" quadrant.

You were faced with a life-threatening disease; you got your medications and did whatever the doctor ordered and now are on the road to recovery. Sure, the body still remains weak and fragile, but you are getting stronger and stronger every-day.

If we take the example of you being in the hole which was discussed a few pages back. You are in the hole. But you have stopped digging the ditch deeper and are now working towards filling the ditch. What do you think is going to happen? Very soon, you will be out of the ditch and the you can start working on building your financial fortress.

If you continue down this path carefully, soon you will be a part of the Gold Class.

The situations which you will typically face if you are in this part of the quadrant will be –

1. Decreasing debt levels.
2. Decreasing credit card dues.
3. Decreasing interest payments and financial charges.
4. Money left in the bank at the end of the month.
5. Increasing investment portfolio and savings.
6. Increasing investment in assets and equipment's.

7. If you are a business, timely payments of statutory dues and taxes, staff salaries and routine expenses.

8. Underutilized working capital limits

9. Timely payment period to vendors and service providers.

Of course, you still have to be very careful. Your financial strength is still weak and any external shock (a large loss or any accident or any other event) may still cripple you financially. You are doing well in terms of managing your day to day expenses, but any unplanned calamity can make you bankrupt. You still cannot bear the brunt of any financial shock.

There can be a situation where your income is just about enough to cover the expenses and there is nothing left over to repay debts or start on the path of savings and investments. I will personally classify you into to the Negative Cash Flow Quadrant as any increase in expenses (which will happen as surely as the sun rising tomorrow morning).

Positive Net Worth and Positive Cash Flow

I personally call this quadrant the GOLD CLASS. You have assets and you are saving and investing a certain portion of your income every month. You have the ability to absorb external shocks – both financial or otherwise – in your personal and business life.

You have the capacity to invest in equipment's, people or any other resource to grow your business. Your increasing investments are also earning more and more with each passing month and hence your cash flow is ever increasing.

People and Businesses in this part of the quadrant will normally experience the following: -

1. Minimal or Nil debt levels.
2. Monthly surplus of cash after all expenses.
3. Increasing investment in assets and equipment's.
4. Increasing investment portfolio and savings.
5. Increasing interest and dividend income.
6. Underutilized working capital limits
7. Timely payment period to vendors and service providers.

This is the end goal, the holy grail of personal or business finance.

Now that you have read about The Financial Position Matrix and also have worked out where you are within the matrix. You also have read through the typical situations a person on each side of the matrix will face. I would strongly urge you to spend some time thinking about your finances (personal or business) and write down your thoughts on the same.

Next, let's have a look at some other important ratios and numbers that one should keep track of to fine tune the financial health.

Key Financial Ratios, Concepts and Terms

This section will simply cover a few more concepts and ratios which you may need to assess your financial position. We will just be covering them in brief here and for any further details or clarifications, you can write in to us to do a simple google search and you should get all the answers.

Liquid Assets to monthly expense ratio (also called the cash runway)

This Formula we use to calculate this ratio is – All Liquid Assets divided by Total Monthly expenses. The resultant number will be the number of months which you can survive in case all your income stops today.

Liquid Assets are essentially a sum total of cash in hand, cash at bank including fixed deposits, your stock market and mutual fund investments, etc. Essentially anything which you can convert into hard cash at a moment's notice. Anything which cannot be liquidated or anything which cannot be liquidated immediately are not to be included in this.

Your monthly expenses are your average expenditure every month. For businesses, since you cannot fire your employees or close down your offices in an instant, please take all expenses as required monthly expenses

We will further explain with a few examples here –

	Example 1	Example 2	Your number
Liquid Assets (A)	1,00,000	5,00,000	
Monthly Expenses (B)	1,25,000	1,25,000	
No of months liquidity or cash available [A/B]	0.8 months	4 months	

Your number should be anywhere between 6 to 9 months to take care of emergencies and any eventualities that may arise.

Active vs passive income / passive income to monthly expenses ratio

This is the number which tells you the percentage of income you have to earn by doing effort vs the income which you earn from your investments. The simple way to classify this income is to ask yourself the question – Will this income continue of I stop working from tomorrow? If the answer is yes, then it is a passive income, otherwise it is active income.

Let's consider what is considered as active and what is considered as passive income –

Active Income	*Passive Income*
Income from salary	*Interest on Bank and corporate deposits*
Income from self-owned small businesses	*Dividend from shares and Mutual funds*
Income from consulting (e.g. doctor's or lawyer's fees)	*Rent from property*
	Royalty
	Income from Medium and large businesses (provided the company can run without you, which it ideally should)

Passive income to monthly expenses ratio is calculated Monthly Passive Income / Monthly Expenses *100.

*The result is the % of your expenses that can be met with current level of passive income. The higher this nu*mber, the better.

Let's look at 2 examples –

	Person A	*Person B*

Total Income	1,00,000	1,00,000
Passive Income	10,000	50,000
Total Monthly Expenses	40,000	40,000
Passive Income to Expense %	25% (10,000/40,000*100)	125% (50,000/40,000*100)

Everyone would obviously want to be in the second situation wherein all your expenses are covered by your passive income and then you have some more leftover to reinvest.

A lot of financial experts out there will also tell you that the day your passive income is more than your monthly expenses, you are financially free and have the choice to retire.

I personally only partially agree to this.

Why I agree to the importance of passive income concept is the multiplier effect that it can have on your income and net worth. Even if your active income grows linearly or remains stagnant, your passive income when reinvested will grow exponentially (the principle of compounding). Also, once your passive income is roughly double your active income, you can then even think of retiring from your present job / active vocation as 200% is a pretty good cover most uncertainties. Also, it's a good feeling to know that you are not dependent on your vocation for your expenses. It's a damn good feeling.

Why I don't agree to the retiring when passive income exceeds income is because of the following 3 reasons: -

1. You cannot accurately predict the way your expenses will grow and hence your current passive income may not be sufficient to cover your expenses in the future.

2. Most of the passive income sources above carry some or the other sort of uncertainty with it: -

    a. Interest on Bank deposits – Much lesser than inflation

      b.   Dividends – uncertain and erratic in terms of when the money comes into your hand. Also, risks of volatility in the markets.

      c.   Rental Income – Vacancy risk

3. I personally believe that you should remain a contributing member of the society for as long as possible, I personally will not like to retire till the time I am able to work and produce. Why be a burden on anyone? Why be a burden on planet earth?

Net Worth to Yearly income Ratio

This is the final number which I will measure and would want you to calculate. As the headline suggests, to calculate this number, you simply divide your net worth from your yearly income.

The resultant number will tell you how many years income have you saved and invested wisely and essentially what you have done financially your whole life.

Let's see 2 examples

	Person A	*Person B*
Total Yearly Income (A)	10,00,000	10,00,000
Net Worth (B)	5,00,000	50,00,000
No of years working (C)	10	10
Net Worth to Income Ratio [B/A]	0.5	5
NW per year worked [B/A]	50,000	5,00,000

You can also conclude from the above that Person B has been much more responsible for his finances as compared to person B. Obviously time also helps in terms of helping your investment grow in value and helping your NW also to grow.

While this number will give you a small measure of how responsible with your money you have been till date, it will also tell you that you now need to change your behavior and your thoughts towards your money.

Debt Servicing Ratio (Income to debt Servicing Ratio)

This is simply the monthly outflow on account of debt in the business (Interest payments + principal payments) divided by the total monthly income. It is normally calculated in % and can range from 0% to more than 100% of your income. Let's understand this with a few examples –

	Person A	*Person B*
Total Monthly Income (A)	1,00,000	1,00,000
Total Monthly Debt Servicing (Installments to Term Loans + Interest on CC/OD Loans+ Other interest) (B)	10,000	75,000
Debt Servicing to Income Ratio (B/A*100)	10%	75%

Obvious conclusions: -

1. Person B is spending way more of his monthly income in servicing debt.
2. Person B, in all likelihood, will not be in a position to save much after considering other living expenses
3. Any emergency expense will put person B more in debt and further harm his cash flows.
4. Any loss of income will again affect person B more than person A.

The Question which you need to ask is – What is your Debt Servicing Ratio? How much of your income is going in servicing debt? How do you feel about it? What will you do about it?

Summary / Key Takeaways

Calculate all the above ratios for you and again spend some time holistically on the numbers you have calculated till now. Look at your cash flows, your net-worth, your placement within the money matrix and the ratios above. They together will tell you everything that you need to know about your financial life till date.

Use the summary table below to get a bird's eye view of your financial position. Please prepare a separate table for your personal and business finances –

Cash Flow (monthly)	Your Inflow / income –	Your Outflow / Expenses	Net Cash Flow
Net Worth	Total assets	Total Liabilities	Net Worth
	Active Income (Amount)	Passive Income (Amount)	Passive Income to Monthly Expense Ratio
	Liquid Assets (amount)	Liquid Expenses to Monthly expense Ratio- _____Months	Net Worth to yearly income ratio – _____times
	Debt Servicing Ratio _____%		

Now that we know where you are, lets dive straight into the actions that you might take to improve and better your present financial position.

PART II: Improving Your Finances

This section will serve as a guidebook to the improvement process. The issues which have been created over a considerable period of time will not go away in a day. There is no magic pill to improving your finances overnight. There is a process which needs to be followed, a regimen which needs to be adhered to and but for sure, you will surely reach the pinnacle of your financial success. Let's dive right in.

Chapter Four: Setting Your Priorities

You are in one particular quadrant of the Money Matrix. Except for the GOLDEN CLASS (Positive Cash flow and positive net worth quadrant), you are probably worried about your finances and are looking at ways and means of improving your finances. There will be a lot of questions now swirling in your head. A lot of thoughts which will need to be put in the order of priority. Let's try and answer a few of them.

What to Tackle First - Cash Flows or Net Worth?

The simple answer is – **Cash Flow is to be tackled first** – Each and Every time.

You need to stop the bleeding, the hemorrhage, before you think of working on building strength. You need to stop digging the hole and start filling it up.

The only way you can build assets without stealing is to have positive cash flows. The Only way you can repay debts is to have positive cash flows. There is no way to increase net worth but to have larger and larger free or positive cash flows.

On the other side, If you are losing money every month, it has to come from somewhere – either through sale of assets or through borrowings. Either way, your net worth is eroding every single day.

So, the first and foremost thing that you should focus on is your cash flows. If they are negative at this point, then getting them to positive. If they are positive, finding ways and means to make them larger and larger.

Increase your income or Reduce Expenses?

Now that our first focus is to increase the cash flows, the obvious next question is – What to I focus on – Reducing expenses or increasing income?

My take on this is that in the absolute short term, reducing expenses is the way to go. But, the better and sustainable way (slightly longer term) if to increase income and finding ways to keep it growing while keeping the expenses in check. I will focus and spend about 80% of my energies in increasing revenues and the balance 20% on reducing expenses and driving efficiencies.

One very important variable is your occupation. If you are a salaried employee, then it will be very difficult to increase your income in the short term. There may be certain vocations which give you commissions related to the sales you bring in or overtime payments. But most of the employees do not really have the commission or overtime option. Finding a new job with better pay also takes time.

For A business, its relatively easier to increase revenues. This can be done by offering additional services to existing customers, or finding newer customers. For a retail business, a little marketing campaign may do the trick. But for a business, it a comparatively easier to scale up revenues.

Looking at the 6-month expense trends (which you have calculated already), will give you a very detailed look at your personal and business expenses. These numbers would have been a revelation and will give you a very good idea in terms of what you can cut down and where you are spending on things where you are wasting money.

Decide on expenses in the following three buckets (for both your personal and business finance) –

1. Essential
2. Important
3. Everything else.

While there is a scope of cutting down expenses in all the categories above, I would suggest that you start by looking at cutting expenses in the third category (not essential and not important expenses) to score some very quick wins.

Some expenses can be reduced immediately – like subscriptions you no longer need, changing your telephone and internet plans, etc. Some expenses like interest expense can be reduced by paying off debts. Look at each expense head and see if you can reduce the same.

For more tips on cutting down expenses, you can do a quick internet search and you will a whole list of tips and tricks to reduce specific expenses.

Save and Invest or Pay off Debts?

The next question is what to do with the surplus cash flow that you have every month. Broadly, you can either save the same and invest it to build assets or you can use it to pay off debts and liabilities.

Both of them have their own merits, but I would suggest the following the following structure and steps to follow: -

1. Build a liquid emergency fund to the tune of 6 months of expenses

2. Once the emergency fund is in place, pay off all high cost debts (A high cost debt is any debt which costs you more than fixed deposits at bank). An exception to this can be your mortgage / housing which you may or may not want to pay off quickly.

3. Once the debts are paid off and you are debt free, look at investing in assets to build additional income streams like rent, interest and dividends.

4. Businesses which are growing may decide to reinvest the monthly surplus in their business as working capital before paying off debts.

5. Mature and stagnant businesses should make repaying debt their priority.

All other things being equal, paying off debts is a good strategy after the emergency funds are in place. The hierarchy of debts should be highest interest first, though a few people like Dave Ramsey also advocate the Smallest balance first method so that you can see some quick emotional victories. Both strategies are good and makes no real difference in the long run as long are you are on track to paying off your debts.

One Source of Income or Multiple Sources of Income?

This is a very interesting question. And the answer to this is very straightforward – Multiple Sources of Income any day is better than one source of Income.

Let's take a few examples –

1. All writers have published multiple books are earning royalties from all of them. Even though technically, they only earn from their writing profession, they have all these books earning money for them individually.

2. A real estate investor may be earning from multiple units and hence is diversified. If you have only one rented unit and it remains unoccupied for an extended period of time, your income is essentially zero. However, if you have 5 units and 1 of them is empty, you still have 80% of your income.

3. Same for your business – If you are dependent on 1 client and you lose that client, your income basically goes to zero. However, if you have 10 clients and you lose one of them, you still have 90% of your income.

   You also have to diversify the services you offer. If you have one service offering and someone else comes up with a way to offer the same at 50% less cost, then you are essentially out of business overnight. However, if you have multiple services, then you can continue to offer other services.

4. As a salaried person, you need to develop other sources of income. It will take time and it will be a slow process. But it can be done. You can look at the following sources of income
   a. Income from rental real estate
   b. Interest on deposits with bank
   c. Dividend income
   d. Royalties on books you own and patents leased out.
   e. Income from part time teaching work.

f. Income from selling home-made products.
g. Advertising Income from your YouTube, Twitter, Instagram and Facebook channels.
h. Income from freelance work – technical work, content writing etc.

This is just a small list of income possibilities which are available out there. Do your research, look around you. You will surely find multiple options.

The Route from Any Quadrant to The GOLD CLASS?

There are basically 2 ways to go from being Bankrupt to being in the best of a financial position. It basically will need you to work on the following 2 parameters –

1. First priority is - If you have negative cash flow, turning that into a positive cash flow.
2. Once cash flows are positive, the looking at converting that negative net worth into a positive net worth.

With the end goal of reaching the GOLD CLASS and Depending on where you are on the financial position matrix, your path can look at any one of the few below: -

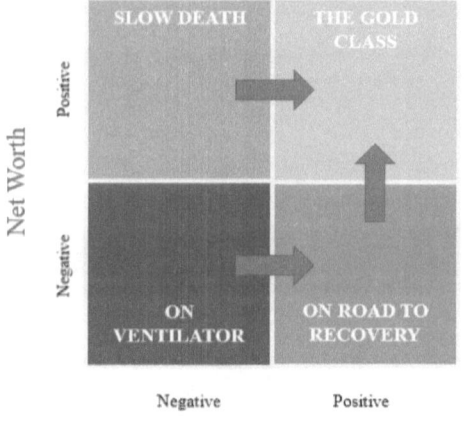

Cash Flow

In the next chapter, lets have a look at specific strategies you can take to improve both your cash flows and your Net Worth. Irrespective of the quadrant you are in, you will need to consistently work on improving your cash flows and subsequently improving your net worth. We will tackle it in this way only – First is how to improve cash flows. And then How to improve your net worth.

Chapter Five: Improving Cash Flows

Cash Flow can improve by doing only 2 things –

1. Reducing your expenses
2. Increasing Your income

Whatever quadrant of the Money Matrix you are in, you need to constantly work on these 2 to keep improving your financial life.

Also, I cannot stress enough on the 2 points below: -

1. Have Faith – Have faith in your own capabilities and the human resilience. People before you have gone through much worse and come out far stronger and better. I am sure you have read about the struggles of some of the superstars in business, literature and any other field. Believe in yourself and believe in Higher Powers.

2. Have a Guide or Mentor with you through the journey – Have a shoulder to cry on. Have a person, a guide, a mentor through these difficult times. He will not only be a sounding board, but will also stop you from making more mistakes and digging the hole even deeper.

When you have Negative Cash Flows, very soon you will find yourself dependent on others even for survival. You may be able to borrow from one to pay another at this point, but there will soon be a point wherein you will not be able to keep the ball rolling and it will all come crashing down. You really need to take some drastic actions and that too immediately.

Following are some actions you can take:

Generating More and More Inflows

Increase your sales - If you are a business owner, it will be a little easier for you to do this. Just go out and start selling (presuming that the product that you sell is profitable at a unit level). If you do not sell today, you will remain hungry. If you do not increase your sales, you will soon have to close your business. No option but to sell. And selling is simple, meet more and more people, get in front of them and tell them about your services. Get out there. Now is not the time to get into a shell and wallow in self-pity. Get out there. Just Go and Sell.

a. **Increase your prices -** You will also have to look at your pricing structure, your product and service mix and your entire business in a holistic way. Sometimes, you have really underpriced the goods and services you sell and the customer may be willing to pay more. When was the last time you had increased your prices? I can bet that you can increase your prices by about 20% in the next 6 months and 90% of the customers will not even blink. The math on this is

	Old	New	
Price per unit	100	120	prices hiked by 20%
No of units sold	100	90	Decreased by 10% due to hike in prices
Total Revenue	**10,000**	**10,800**	

You can see above, by increasing prices, you actually stand to gain.

Of course, there can be a chance that you cannot increase prices (yours is a commodity product), in that case better efficiencies and more sales volumes is the way to go.

b. **Cut Out Low Margin and Non-Performing Products and Services** – As a business practice, every six months you should do a review of the services that you offer and cut out the bottom 25% of the products and services which are of low margins and which do not sell. I personally recommend 25% as it will make you think long and hard about each product and service and how you can improve the margins on it or increase its sales. If you are not comfortable with 25%, you can cut out the bottom 10%.

> *Increase in sales is a function of increase in number units sold, the price at which it is sold and the margin on each sale. If you have addressed all three and increased the number of products you sell, increased the realization or sales value per product and improved the margins on each, you have just supercharged your business. Congratulations.*

If you are a salaried person working for someone else, then it's a little more difficult for you. But not impossible. There are multiple things which you can do to earn a little more.

a. You can write a book.

b. You can take tuitions.

c. You can make a product and sell it though the local stores.

d. You can do online affiliate marketing.

e. You can take online courses.

f. You can teach part time at a business college or a coaching center.

g. You can make websites for others after office hours (if you have the skill).

h. If you are good at baking, start baking and selling cupcakes and birthday cakes.

i. Start a home tiffin service.

j. Write a blog or make a YouTube channel and earn from google advertisements.

k. Offer consulting services to others if the company where you work permits.
l. Rent out the spare bedroom on AirBnB or to students as paying guest.

Look around and you will find a way.

Your sales and revenues have been increasing steadily. Do you really need this laser focus on selling more? Should You still sell, sell and then sell some more?

The simple Answer is Yes. It does not matter what is your financial position today. If you are not passionate about growing your business and are not excited to reach and serve more and more customers, you should probably not be in it. Better to sell the business to someone and then go out and do something else.

If you have a job, it should excite you, every Monday you should be going to office with a spring in your step. Only then it is worth it. After all, we all get only one life.

Reducing Outflows

When you are in the negative net worth, negative cash flow quadrant, you do not have the comfort of business or personal assets and things can go from bad to worse in matter of days. At this stage you have to spend at 50% of your time on increasing sales and the balance 50% on cost and process controls.

You have to be Brutal and absolutely ruthless in reducing operational and discretionary expenses. Any expense that is not absolutely critical has to be deferred, reduced and totally avoided. This may mean no holidays, taking the public transport instead of your own vehicle, no expense which is not absolutely critical.

As a business in the worst possible quadrant and your business on probably its last legs, you should also look at downsizing your business and reworking and reshaping your business processes. The Biggest 2 expense heads which a business has are salaries and rent. You should start by focusing on these two.

a. Do more with lesser number of people. If needed, reduce the workforce by 50% and give the balance a 25% hike. This will not only reduce the manpower expenses, but also encourage the remaining team to do more and turn around the business.

b. Cut down fixed overheads like rental by moving into a smaller space (if you can manage that). This will immediately give you a fixed savings in expense every month. You can also cut down on other overheads like travel etc. by better planning, using economy instead of business class, etc. Small changes like Moving from brand name coffee to generic but equally good coffee can also help.

As your situation improves and when you move from being on a ventilator to the recovery room and then to the Gold Class, your approach to your finance will change. You should start giving more and more time on increasing sales and lesser time on reducing costs.

c. As you improve your cash flows and get in a better position, shift your focus from reducing employee count to increasing efficiencies and employee productivity. This is a better way in the longer term. It is with your team that you can grow quickly.

d. Invest in software and automation so that you can further improve efficiencies and reduce your dependency on people. Its oxymoronic to mention investment in a section focusing on reducing debt. But yes, this is placed here intentionally. Investing in systems, processes and infrastructure eventually help you save a lot of money in terms of reduced errors, more productivity and better efficiencies.

This does not mean that you start spending freely again or you waste money and resources. You still run a tight ship, but your focus is on steering the ship to its destination while still maintaining good cost controls.

Please also note that, I am not saying that you should not enjoy the finer things in life. If you want to travel, you should. If you want to buy expensive watches, you should. If you like cars, you should absolutely have a collection. The only thing is, everything should be done at an appropriate time. Once you can afford to spend your money on these, by all means, please do. But till the time you have built your financial fortress, please have the common sense to know what your financials can afford and what they cannot.

Reduce Interest Costs

Most of the businesses and people out there are married to debt and interest. They keep paying interest on one thing or the other to bankers and lenders making them very rich in the process. Sometimes, it's for the car, sometimes it's the house, sometimes it's for medical emergencies. Most of the times, it's for some silly purchases on a credit card.

Interest and debt obligations are one of the top 3 items in the monthly outflow and expense list (In about 50% of the cases, it is the largest).

Looking at the cash flow statement prepared before, what % of your income are you spending on interest and debt servicing obligations? Now imagine if that money was available to you in your hand to as you please. That amount invested for your retirement. Wouldn't that be great?

Reducing interest outflows can be done in the following 2 ways:

1. Refinancing your existing debt to a lower rate debt and better terms –

    Self-explanatory. This helps you in reducing the interest paid as well as the overall cash outflows (most of the times, it is lower than before).

2. Second is to simply pay off the current debt and not borrowing more.

    It's a little bit of a chicken and egg story. You have to have surplus cash flows to repay debt and reduce interest outflows. And then you have to pay off debt to reduce interest outflows and improve cash flows further. But once you start down this path, it becomes a self-enforcing system wherein the more debt you repay, the more cash you will have in hand from reduced interest outflows to further pay down the debt faster.

There is enough information out there on how to repay debts faster. We will discuss a few pointers in brief in the Next section of the book.

That's all about improving your cash flows. As you can see, cutting expenses will only get you so far and no further. Increasing Sales and Increasing Income is the way to go and should be the primary go to strategy in 90% of the cases. This should however, be supported by a cost control and efficiency strategy.

Now that we have worked on our cash flows and got them into positive territory and are working on increasing them with each passing day. It is imperative to know what to do with this surplus and how to get to a comfortable and eventually a huge net worth. That is what is being covered in the next chapter.

Chapter Six: Improving Net Worth

Net Worth is just made up of assets and liabilities. The basic action will be to increase assets and decreasing liabilities. There is no other formula out there. There are a few actions mentioned below which you can take.

The thing which you will need is to have a positive cash flow to do either reduce debt or acquire more assets. We will talk about the 2 below. First, the repaying debt part and the second is increasing assets.

Reducing Liabilities

Reducing liabilities essentially is taking all or a part of your surplus cash flows and put it towards repaying the personal and business debts that you have.

A few things which you need to know before you make your debt repayment plan are –

- Does your lender allow for pre-payment or partial pre-payment? – For example, In India, you cannot make a partial pre-payment on a car loan or a personal loan and have the option of full foreclosure only. You can however, make a partial payment on your housing loan and a loan against property / mortgage loan.

- What are the prepayment charges involved? – Some have no penalty (like your housing loan) while others charge foreclosure penalty (range between 2 to 5 percent of the outstanding loan amount). Calculate this foreclosure amount and then take an informed call on the prepayment of that loan.

So, what systems do people use while prepaying debt? The general financial wisdom prevalent in the public gives us the following ways and means to tackle debt.

1. Refinancing and Loan Consolidation

The first thing to do is to look at the option of refinancing and restructuring your existing debts in order to reduce interest. Paying off high interest loans like credit cards and unsecured loans using refinancing (taking finance against your house or car) will significantly shorten the timeline needed to repay debts.

A lot of financial advisors out there do not suggest refinance, but if you can save 4%-10% on some debts by refinancing, then I very strongly suggest that you do the same.

Let's look at an example

Loan Type	outstanding amount	rate of interest (per annum)	monthly interest paid
Home Loan	25,00,000	9%	18,750
Credit Card	5,00,000	36%	15,000
Total Interest Paid			**33,750**
After Refinancing			
Home Loan	25,00,000	9%	18,750
Top Up on Home Loan	5,00,000	12%	5,000
Total Interest Paid			**23,750**
Savings in interest per month			**10,000**
Savings %			29.8%

This additional savings in the debt repayments can be used for faster repayments or for savings and investments depending on your priorities.

You are actually saving money as this interest payment otherwise will be an expense (which is converted into an asset by either adding to your assets or repaying liabilities).

Now that you have done consolidation and reduced your interest outflows and you have calculated your cash flows and know what surplus you can use towards prepayment of debt. Let's look at the 2 prevalent methods used by people for prepaying debt.

2. Paying Highest Interest First

The most logical and mathematically correct way of repaying debts is to list them down in the order of their interest rates and then start paying it off in highest interest rate to lower interest rate order. As the name suggests, it help you in minimizing your interest outflows by ensuring that you are paying off the loans which are costing you more every month.

Once the highest loan is gone, you take that amount and use it towards the loan with the next highest rate of interest. And the process continues till the time all the debt is paid off.

Mathematically, the most efficient method which will ensure that you will repay all your debts with the least possible interest outflows.

3. The Lowest Amount of Debt first / Debt Snowball method

This is where you will start paying debts not in the order of their interest rates, but in the order of smaller to bigger. You will list your debt as smallest first and start putting your surplus towards that debt till the time it is repaid. Once that is closed, you will now then take all the surplus (including the money you were using to pay towards the debt you just closed) and start paying off the next smallest debt.

This method essentially pays on Human Psychology and gives you some very quick wins. These debts going knocked off liabilities gives you a sort of morale boost that further spurs you on.

Though not very sound mathematically (you will pay higher interest as compared to the highest interest first method), it is nevertheless recommended for most of people out there simply because of the quick wins that it offers.

You can do a quick google search for "Debt Snowball" for further reading.

Increasing Your Assets

Now you have understood the importance of positive monthly cash flows. You have also understood the concept of debt repayments. Sooner or later, you will decide to start using this monthly cash flow and start building assets with it. You have to make the important decision of how to deploy the money you are earning so that you make the most of it.

How are assets classified? Are all assets Equal? It's a very important portion of your financial life and a whole book can be written on the subject of how to invest (and indeed, many books have been written on the subject too). In the following pages, we will try and cover a few basics and give you a primer in terms of how to take that decision.

1. Asset Classifications.

a. Appreciating vs Depreciating Assets

Asset which rise in value with passage of time are called appreciating assets. Example will be your real estate (most of the times)

Assets which go down in value with passage of time are depreciating assets. Example – Your Car or your Boat, your mobile phone, your office computers the furniture you own etc.

One should avoid buying depreciating assets as much as possible. It feels good to upgrade your car every 3 years, but it does nothing at all towards increasing your Net worth. Instead of buying that 20-lac car, buy a small shop on the outskirts of the city which will not only appreciate in value, but also give you rental income.

Of course, if your current car is now not worth keeping, then by all means upgrade. But don't upgrade just for the heck of it. Same for other purchases like Televisions, Mobile Phones, Gadgets, etc.

b. Liquid vs Illiquid Assets

Assets which can be converted to cash easily (1 – 3 days times) are known as liquid assets. Your money in the bank, your deposits, your mutual fund investments, etc. are all examples of liquid assets.

All assets which cannot be converted into cash within that period are illiquid assets. Example will be your house, your investment real estate, your car, etc. Assets like the value of your holding in your own business is also illiquid as it cannot be readily converted into cash.

c. Income earning vs Non-Income Earning Assets

Assets which put money in your pocket every month are income earning assets. A same class of asset can be a part of both classifications. For example, the house you live in is not an income earning asset. However, the house you have rented out is an income earning asset.

d. Safe vs. At Risk Assets

Assets whose value does not fluctuate every day and where your capital is protected are safe assets. These include money in the bank, Fixed deposits at banks, investment in government bonds, etc. Normally, these offer a very low return on investment which generally does not even keep pace with inflation.

Investments in equity mutual funds, investments in shares of companies, stocks in hand etc. are at risk assets as their values fluctuate every day with the mood of the market's they trade in. These offer better returns in the longer term, but can be very volatile in shorter periods. At this point, we have seen the NIFTY 50 go down from 12,000 all the way to 7500 and then back again to 9000. All within a space of 25-30 days. That was a 40% drop from the peaks within a month can be scary. However, over the last 10 years, it has consistently given a 15% annual compounded return.

2. Ideal Asset Mix:

You have to decide what your ideal asset mix should be. However, all deployment of surplus cash flows towards purchase of assets should pass the following filters: -

a. Do I need this money in the next 12-24 months? If yes, then deploy in short term liquid assets only.
b. If I do not need this money in the next 12-24 month, then is it an appreciating asset? If no, then Do I really need it?
c. Is this an income earning asset? If not, what is the purpose of buying this?

The ideal asset mix that you or your business should have will be very specific to your specific situation in life. For me the ideal asset mix will be –

Asset Mix	Age		
	25-45	45-60	60+
Real Estate (self-Occupied)	40%	30%	20% or less
Real Estate (rented out)	0	30%	40%
Mutual Funds / Stocks	50%	30%	15%
Liquid Funds	10%	10%	25%

With age, you should reduce the contribution of at-risk assets (like equity mutual funds and stocks) in your portfolio and replace them with safe, income earning assets. I would suggest that you sit with your financial advisor and then draw up the asset mix which will suit your requirements and principles in life.

Selling Assets to Repay Liabilities

One very common question is – I have made this asset with great difficulties and I do not want to sell it to repay liabilities. Valid Question, and also a very deep emotional connect with many people (specially when it comes to real estate).

What I believe is that the intensity of asset sale should be in directly proportional to the debt servicing capacity of your inflows. The higher % of your inflows going towards debt servicing, the more you should look at disposing assets to pay off liabilities.

You have already calculated this number earlier. If it is more than 60% of your monthly income is being used for servicing debt, then you should start liquidating your assets to reduce the debt load. If the number is less than 30%, then asset disposal can be optional and the primary focus should be repayment through cash flows.

Which Assets to Liquidate?

Look at the list of assets you have made earlier. Then Add to it all the other things which can be sold for some money (clothes which do not wear, the bicycle which is gathering dust in parking, furniture which you do not use, old mobile phones in the drawer, 2nd and 3rd Television Set at home, the extensive library of hardcover books that you have – just list everything.

Depending on the criticality of your financial position, Sell some / all of them on Quikr, craigslist, or any other online sites where you can sell these.

Liquidate all the dead and slow-moving inventory by offering deep discounts or even selling them to scrap merchants.

An indicative hierarchy of asset sales is: -
1. All assets which you have not used for 6 months or more including dead stock in business.

2. All Depreciating assets (not being used / rarely used) like old office and factory equipment's, your unused treadmill, etc.
3. Investment real estate.
4. Investments in Mutual Funds and Stocks.
5. Self- owned real estate.

I strongly suggest selling everything you have not used for the last 6 months. Not only will it free up some capital, it will also help you declutter your space which then can be used more efficiently.

Significant amounts of cash can be raised by downsizing your car (if not an outright sale and using public transport for commuting).

If you are in very difficult situation, you should also consider selling your office / residence / both and free up the capital. This will also help you to reduce your monthly cash outflow in terms of the Monthly Installments (even considering the additional rent expense that you will incur).

Repaying Liabilities (even by selling assets) will help you to reduce your outflows dramatically. For a lot of people this will do the trick and immediately move your cash flows from negative to positive. You may think that you are now less secure than before as you do not have assets to back you, but that's simply not true.

With monthly shortfalls, and you having already borrowed against your assets, you would have soon started defaulting on your loans. It is only a matter of time before the banks take the asset away from you. When Banks and lenders sell the asset, more often than not it is sold at a discount At least when you will sell it yourself, you will be able to sell it a better price and you will get to keep everything you realize over and above the loan/debt outstanding against the asset.

Epilogue/Conclusion

I would again like to end this with a few quotes from Arthshashtra – the ancient Indian treatise of Economics written by Chanakya –

अर्थेषणा न व्यसनेषु गण्यते।
Longing for amassing wealth is not an addiction.
Since it could be deserve of nearly all. Everyone wants to be rich!

वृत्तिमूलमर्थलाभः।
Gain is the basic aim of any endeavor
All work to gain some kind of benefit which is the aim of every profession as well.

कार्यान्तरे दीर्घसूत्रता न कर्तव्या।
Be not slack before the whole job is finished.
Lazing mid-way at work, one may not finish it well or timely.

दैवं बिनाऽति प्रयत्नं करोति यत्तद्द्विपफलम्।
God helps those who help themselves.

अलब्धलाभादिचतुष्टयं राज्यतन्त्रम्।
It is essential for a state to ensure four inaccessible gains
To get what it doesn't have
To ensure its security after it is gained
To ensure growth in that asset thus gained
To swap that gain with something more advantageous to the state

These were the teachings of our heritage, our culture. Yes, you should aspire for wealth. You have to work hard for it. And once you work get it, you should look at its growth and safety.

There is no magic formula, no genie who can magically take all your financial problems away. There is only a lot of blood, sweat and hard work.

No-one else can help you with your financial problems. It is a lonely journey which you have to make on your own. The support of your loved ones during this journey will make it easier, but you are the own who has to make it happen.

I have time and again seen people overcome great odds and come out successful. With this small book, we have tried to give you a framework within which you can make sense of your finances and start on the journey to building your financial fortress.

And your reading this book tells me that you want to be successful financially. Go out, start the journey, pay your dues in hard work and efforts and nothing can stop you.

About the Author

The Author started his career in Sales with Bharat petroleum Corporation Limited selling Lubricants in 2003 and then switching to financial sector in 2004. He has worked with ICICI Bank and Reliance Capital, predominantly in the lending side of business and has handled large teams and geographies.

He currently has his own Boutique Investment Banking Firm since 2013. He also is involved in turning around a large restaurant chain in western India as its consulting CFO and made it profitable within a span of 15 months.

Over the last 17 years, He has studied and assessed financials of over 5000 small and medium sized corporates across industries and geographies and is involved in loans of over 5000 Crs.

His current startup is one in the finance space providing analytics to restaurants and helping them with data driven decision making.

He is an MBA from NMIMS and currently resides in Pune with his family and 6 pets.

You can read more about Saurabh at his businesses at

https://www.linkedin.com/in/saurabhprofile/

www.devmaheshwari.com

www.fnbanalytica.com.

The author can be reached at sm@devmaheshwari.com

www.ingramcontent.com/pod-product-compliance
Lightning Source LLC
Chambersburg PA
CBHW021500210526
45463CB00002B/821